AN

MASTERING THE ART OF MALE SUPREMACY

TRAINING TECHNIQUES FOR THE HOME FRONT

Illustrations by Steve Soeffing

PALADIN PRESS
BOULDER, COLORADO

Mastering the Art of Male Supremacy:
Training Techniques for the Home Front
by Andy Kane

Copyright © 1986 by Andy Kane

ISBN 10: 0-87364-386-0
ISBN 13: 978-0-87364-386-3

Printed in the United States of America

Published by Paladin Press, a division of
Paladin Enterprises, Inc.,
Gunbarrel Tech Center
7077 Winchester Circle
Boulder, Colorado 80301 USA
+1.303.443.7250

Direct inquiries and/or orders to the above address.

Visit our Web site at www.paladin-press.com

Illustrations by Steve Soeffing

Contents

This book is dedicated to my first wife, Evelyn, and backups, Barb, Kathy, Diane, Maryann, April, Barbara, Robin I, Paula, Sheri, Denise, Gloria, Joanne, Pat, Doreen, Donna, Angel, Cindy, Lori, Nancy, and Robin II. I couldn't have done it without you!

Preface

First of all, let me put all of the women libbers, feminists and do-gooders to rest by saying that I don't condone violence in training a wife—maybe a rolled-up newspaper on the rump once in a while, but no real violence. Besides violence is not the best way. It only worked for the cavemen because there were no alternate methods back in those days.

We now have many alternative methods available that do not involve brute force. There are conversation, bribery with gifts, shunning, psychological warfare, tantrums and many other goodies to use in place of the club, and they all work better than the club!

Violence is a "no-no," so you feminists can go back to your picketing of nuclear arms plants or whatever.

Why is a training manual necessary? Simple. . . unless you are a Class-A Wimp and want your life managed by a skirt for the rest of your life, you must train your mate from the very beginning. Every corporation, every business, every organization, every country has only one real boss. The reason most marriages or live-in unions don't succeed is because there are two bosses. Every decision ends up in a battle, compromise or dispute. It's much easier to have just one decision-maker and obviously that decision-maker should be you—the man!

Look at it this way. You want to go to a football game (stock car race, wrestling, etc.), and your wife wants to go to the opera (show, church, etc.). You are the boss. You tell her to load the beer cooler and put it in the car. If she is trained well, she obeys, and you both go to the game and have a real swell time.

1

If you don't train her, an argument ensues and you have to carry your own cooler, you're late for the game and you have a rotten time. Training is very important!

When do you start training? *Now!* Training, as with a puppy or kitten, must be begun as early as possible. The first date is a good time to start. A friend of mine, after his wedding ceremony, gave his bride a kiss and a bus token and told her to take a bus home. He came home three days later! Now that's a good way to start the training!

It's never too late. Another friend of mine started vigorously training his mate after they were married ten years. They say, "You can't teach an old dog new tricks," but he was successful. It is harder to do it later, but it can be done. Never give up.

Obviously the best time for training is early, but even if you start late and only accomplish a minor revision in your mate's habits, it will be beneficial. If you are only successful in getting her trained to do one thing each day and you are with her twenty years, that amounts to 7,300 things that will make your life better!

This book should be marked CLASSIFIED or TOP SECRET because it is for male eyes only. If the ladies start reading this it will be counterproductive, since they may recognize the scams before you can pull them off, and also may offer some resistance.

Read on for a more enjoyable life . . .

The Right Stuff

Planning is important in any venture and it is especially important when you consider that the mate you choose may possibly be with you for many moons. If you have been fortunate enough to grab this book before you decide to select a mate, the following tips will greatly enhance your future.

Size and Shape

If you remember when you purchased your last jalopy, there were options, colors, engine sizes, special tires, AM/FM radio, air conditioning, etc. You spent hours considering these options, and you were only going to keep those wheels for 36 months!

Now you a picking a female you may possibly use ten times as long as the Detroit iron. Would you believe that many guys don't have specs for this acquisition? They think that when the right one comes along, bells will ring, and a little white dove with a rose in its beak will fly down, or maybe they will find a shoe that will fit some fair maiden. Fairy tales are made for fairies. Don't believe a word of this romantic garbage.

You must decide what you want now and go after it. When I was contemplating settling down, I made a list of the qualifications I wanted, had my secretary type it up, and then I dated only those girls who fit the description. It was similar to interviewing someone for a job, but you have to use a bit of finesse so she doesn't know that she is being interviewed.

Don't subject the applicant to the third degree. "Did you graduate from college?" "Do you have big tits?"

3

"How much do you weigh?"

You have to camouflage the questions, so the chick is caught off guard. Try this: "I love your blue eyes; did you go to college?" "That's a lovely jacket you are wearing; do you have big tits?" "Let's go sky diving; how much do you weigh?"

I even considered making a plywood template of the dimensions I was looking for in a "broad," and then making sure each possible candidate could pass through before I would take her out.

Some of the ideal qualifications that I used were:

1. Tall—this is important if you are also tall. Nothing looks worse than a 6'9" geek strolling down the lane with a 4'6" dwarf. Conversely, if you are short, nothing looks more ridiculous than walking with a giantess.

2. Blonde—blondes have more fun! If the blonde is having fun and you're with her, you will also have fun.

3. Good body—a must! A lean, well-proportioned body is nice to have in the sack next to you each night. If she has all the other qualifications, except a perfect body, consider sending her in for plastic surgery, implants, etc.

4. Background—family, up-bringing, etc. You should check out her parents for anything that may be hereditary or communicable. VD, AIDS, insanity, and other diseases or traits could ruin your happy home life. It's strange but when you buy a puppy, you get a pedigree going back ten generations and a health certificate from the vet, and the next thing you know, the mutt runs away in six months, or gets squashed by a truck in the street! When you take delivery of your female mate, she's in "as-is" condition, and may never run away or get squashed by a truck! You could have this pet for 30 years, and pay a fortune in vet—I mean doctor—bills. *Check 'em out first!*

5. Education—unless you're a dope, you sure don't want a dope hanging around. If your chick thinks a cul-de-sac is a group of religious fanatics, instead of a road with a turn-around at the end, she could easily embarrass you in public. My requirements are that any prospective partner have some college, or equivalent training, under her bonnet.

6. Personality—keep in mind that you are going to have to spend several hours a day with this bimbo. If,

when the two of you are together, there are any clashes, or if your personalities just do not mesh, maybe you should keep looking. Evaluate the situation carefully. If there appears to be hope that her personality can be altered with your help, you may want to give her a trial run.

My guidelines may not work for everyone. Some guys actually enjoy having a mean, miserable chick around. Some like fat ones. I once was driving a client of mine out to look at a shack he was considering making his abode. We passed a girl on a bicycle (at least I think there was a bicycle under her!) who from the rear resembled the Goodyear blimp at port. If there was a society for the prevention of cruelty to ten-speed bicycles, I think they would have had her arrested.

When we passed this girl, I closed my eyes because I have an easily upset stomach. My crazy client, whom I will call Dimko because that's his real name, hollered out the window, clapped his hands, whistled, jumped up and down and asked me to drive around the block so he could see her again!

Dimko was not fat himself. In fact, he was a good-looking dude. I thought he was kidding at first, but he was insistent that we circumnavigate the block for one more look at the tons of fun. Since he was about to buy a pad from me and I would make six grand in commission, I readily complied.

Our second trip past this hulk produced the same reaction from Dimko. He eventually bought the house I was pushing, and at the closing, I had the "pleasure" of meeting Dimko's bride. She was the spitting image of the bicycle breaker! He really liked huge mamas.

Dimko later confided that he felt sorry for me after seeing my frail (36-21-36) wife. He really likes fat ones. I even heard him say that a fat one comes in handy because she can keep you warm in the winter and produce enough shade in the summer to keep you cool.

I'm sure you get the idea. Make a specification sheet for the chick that will fit your ideas, and then stick to your specs.

This country is full of various-sized dames and you can have your pick. It's a nice country we live in . . . God bless America!

The Black Book

Many guys ceremoniously burn their little black book on the eve of their wedding. Are they nuts or what?

Why should you burn your book? This gesture is done thousands of times each year to signify to the new bride that the groom has given himself to her alone. But you probably spent several grand and many a bad night compiling this list of "10s," and it's a crime to scrap it. You should also not make a present of it to your best man. Keep it, computerize it, copy it, or do whatever you need to make it available later if your wife has a "headache." If you want to burn it to appease her, that's okay, as long as you have the important data squirreled away for a rainy day.

If the bride is a logical girl, you might try this one. Mention that you are considering selling real estate part-time (or pots and pans, insurance, etc.), and these girls in your black book are all of the marrying and settling-down age. They can easily become good clients if you maintain their friendships. (Hee, hee, hee, ha, ha!) You might even invite them all to your wedding reception, so your wife will get used to seeing your old flames around. My wedding reception looked like an old-flames reunion and they gave me some nice wedding gifts besides (except for a sore-loser or two who gave me nicely wrapped rat poison).

Whatever you do, don't eliminate old girlfriends. There is absolutely no reason to ditch them just because they are female. Your male friends will still be around, so it would defy logic to eliminate the females, just because they are female; besides there are federal regulations that forbid sexual discrimination. Keep 'em around!

Grocery Shopping

For some reason many women think their men should stop and shop on the way home from the mill. Guys, your time is too valuable to spend in the supermarket. Groceries are heavy: six or seven bags can total 100 pounds. Shopping is a better job for the lady. Lifting those bags will give her good pectoral muscles, the bending over will keep her belly flat, and you can spend the hour or so that would be required to do the shopping in some bar, watching wrestling on a big screen TV.

How do you train your wife not to ask you to do the shopping or ever be involved in the shopping trip? There are two good methods. You realize, of course, that you can't just say "no" or she will pout and shout. You must appear to be willing, but do so in a manner that will convince her that she should not recruit you again in the near future.

The first method is the togetherness method. You lovingly go along to shop together. As soon as you enter the store, mention that you only have $63.51 with you. This will mentally restrain her from extravagant purchases. As you proceed in the store, you will notice a definite traffic pattern. Possibly it will travel across the front of the store and then down the produce aisle, up the beans, down the soup, up the toilet paper, down the frozen food, up the bakery aisle and to the cashier. You will notice that 99 percent of the zombies follow this pattern. You should immediately go back across the front of the store to the bakery aisle and proceed down that aisle—a reverse pattern. It's something like going the wrong way on a one-way street, only a lot more fun, because you will get to meet every nice-looking girl in

10

the store by following this wisely planned path.

If you travel the regular route, and Miss Nude World is already in the store and two aisles ahead of you, she will always be ahead of you. You will miss seeing those 48 double Ds up close (and maybe even lose the chance of bumping into them!).

OK. Now we have you headed in the right direction. Your loved one is carefully putting items into the wire cart with the $63.51 limit in mind. As you reach the suds aisle, deposit a case of your favorite brew in the cart with great glee. She will give you a funny look because she was watching pennies by buying the generic tuna fish that's only fit for a starving alley-cat, and you just wiped out all her savings with one fell swoop. Don't pay any attention to her. Throw in a giant can of beer nuts for good measure. As you pass through the magazine aisle, grab a $4.50 girlie magazine, flip it open and say "WOW" about four times, real loud.

If you encounter any friends—as you usually do in a neighborhood store—and you stop to chat, stand near your mate and gently pat her on the ass all the time she is talking to Minister Holier-Than-Thou and his wife.

As you proceed through the store and your chick deposits a few items in the buggy that are unnecessary (tampons, toilet paper, bread, milk, etc.), carefully and secretly put them back on the shelf when she is not looking. For good measure, you should run the cart over her toes at least twice during this expedition. When it is time to leave, scout the checkout counter until you find the best-looking cashier. *Don't* look for the shortest line, just the best-looking cashier! When the old lady says, "What the hell are we doing in this line; the one over there is shorter," tell her this cashier is the best looking.

When the order is rung up and it comes to $68.97, look at your woman and ask, "What shall we put back?" She will look at the case of suds and the girlie books. Before she can utter a word, grab the butter or bacon.

When you get the goodies home and she realizes that you declared as unnecessary some of the items she deemed important, explain that you didn't think milk was necessary because you had plenty of beer.

This scheme is guaranteed, and I have never heard of a gal asking her old man to go shopping with her twice if he followed my plan.

In scenario number 2, your mate sends you to the store with a list. This list will contain several important items. If you return from this scavenger hunt with all of the items, you will not be a winner. Instead, you will have demonstrated your ability to follow her orders and return with the right things. But you can't just get all the wrong things because she'll know it's a ruse. If the list says chicken-noodle soup, she will expect the regular two-bowl size can. Get the one-gallon size used for families of fifteen and tell her you did it to save money. If it says "loaf of bread," get day-old, one-half price bread and say, "What's the difference; if I got fresh bread, it would be a day old tomorrow anyway." If it says "onions," buy a one-hundred-pound bag. In a week the sprouts will crowd your lady right out of the kitchen. You get the idea.

This system has really worked for me. At one time I

lived year-round in a summer resort area on the Great Lakes. Many winter storms would strand and isolate my neighbors and myself for days at a time. During one of the ferocious storms that cut us off from civilization for a week, the local police came to check on us, riding a snowmobile and pulling a toboggan. They offered to transport one person the six miles into town to get supplies for the entire group.

The neighbors selected me because I was young and strong and drunk. The grocery-shopping job entailed being dragged on that damn toboggan through swirling snow in ten-degree weather with a windchill factor of negative 29 degrees! If I did a good job of getting the baby formula, the gruel, the creamed corn for my 90-year-old neighbor with no teeth and the dog food for the neighbor's dog who was already licking his chops and eyeing a three-year-old brat, I could see myself being the permanent stooge for the arctic ride every time we were snowed in.

I collected all the money from the neighbors and all their lists, which I carefully folded up and tucked in my parka. Then I took off with Sergeant Preston. At the store I garnered five cases of beer and twelve quarts of liquor which I wisely repacked in soup cases, so the Mountie would not realize he was making the largest booze run of the winter instead of a mercy mission for the starving fools at Lighthouse Beach.

The 90-year-old starved, the dog ate the three-year-old, and needless to say, I was never asked to go to the store again. In fact, some of the neighbors never spoke to me again. (I had a good party though!)

Rags

One thing women cannot resist (besides myself) is clothes. They must have the latest in rags even if it makes them look ridiculous. I have always believed that fashion designers have a secret desire to make women look as foolish as possible. They call it style, but anyone who has half a brain can recognize it as just plain awful.

I personally cannot hold back a big laugh whenever I see an otherwise good-looking girl dressed in seven layers of camouflage with a tow-chain for a belt, hair looking as if she just jumped out of an electric chair, one-foot-long earrings, shoes with heels resembling those of an army nurse, gaudy makeup and a purse made out of a used flour sack—all this in the name of fashion. The ensemble cost her two and one-half weeks secretarial pay, and she ends up looking like a freak.

I think—and I'm sure 99 percent of the guys in the USA agree—that a girl looks best *naked*, i.e., no clothes. A pair of high heels ($5.95) would not hurt. Add a bikini, or a bra and panties (ten bucks), and she still looks real good. Now we have a chick who will appeal to almost all guys, and she only spent $16 on her wardrobe, not $655.95!

If you have any doubt regarding my observations, let's wrap all the contestants in next year's Miss Nude World contest in army blankets and see what the attendance figures are compared to the past contests.

What I'm getting at is that you have to keep a watchful eye on what your chick feels is necessary to keep her warm. You have to decide how *you* want her to look, and then you cannot allow her to even own one piece of clothing that does not fit into your master plan. This

15

is a very important area of the training!

Most guys like their lady to look provocative and appeal to all the other guys with the knowledge that after the game, party, orgy, etc., she will be going home with you.

If the old lady has a favorite sweatshirt that's two sizes too big, try using it to wax the truck next weekend. If she goes grocery shopping and you are home alone, clean out her closet of any sexless garments or things you don't particularly like, and bag them up. Find the nearest Salvation Army depot or Volunteers of America headquarters and take them in. They will give you a donation receipt of the approximate resale value, and you can take this as a deduction on your federal income tax next year.

If your chick screams and yells when she gets home about her favorite sweat pants and old sweater from junior high, tell her you saw a TV spot about refugees, and you just felt compelled by your inner-self to immediately help these freezing people, so you donated some of her bulky, out-of-style, warm clothes to the cause!

If she is still upset, offer to get her something new! Look up the closest Fredericks of Hollywood, or the equivalent, and take her over there.

Here is another one that works well when you are training your lady to dress to please you. You are going to a party or dinner and your mate has dressed in something you do not find pleasing, to say the least! Maybe it's baggy. Grab her and hug and kiss her. Then say, "Why didn't you tell me?" She says, "Huh?" Say, "Why didn't you tell me you were expecting!" She will change fast. Or maybe her dress is too long. Say, "Just today, Bill said he never saw such nice legs, and I know he's going to be disappointed." Presto—she finds a mini. The trick is to not just say, "You look like crap!" You have to use subterfuge. If she really looks bad and refuses to change, you should just stay home and watch TV. Next time she will look ravishing without any assistance or prodding.

You should always make it a point to go with her when she shops for rags. If you're not there, some pushy salesgirl will probably send her back with the exact same crap you donated to the Salvation Army!

Birthing

You're not going to believe this, but in the past few years, the feminists and nature nuts have decided that your work is *not* done after you knock up your chick. They want you around nine months later to help breathe, grunt, push, hiccup, scream and yell, and get splashed with debris in the delivery room!

Don't they know that this is counterproductive? There are better things you could be doing. The proud father does not belong in the delivery room wrapped up in a blue cape. His sacred duty is to be out buying a box of cigars and getting drunk at the closest topless bar.

I always looked forward to my wife going in to deliver the latest brat. It gave me a couple of nights out to fondle a dancer or two, and tie a good one on. Now, not only does your mate want you there for the grand finale, but she wants you there for the practice sessions, too. These consist of going to a group class with ten or twelve other repulsive-looking chicks with fat bellies to practice breathing, grunting and pushing.

Here's how you handle it. Act interested. When you go to the first session and the tubs of lard start grunting and groaning, pass out! Fall over and refuse to awaken. Make them revive you with all their techniques. When you try to stand up, go rubberlegged again and require assistance from the ladies. If no one is looking, stick your finger down your throat and puke, preferably on the instructor, or another one of the bubble bellies.

Tell your chick that you just can't take the sound of pain. You can bet that after your Academy Award performance, you will not be invited to any more of the practice sessions!

Let's all stick together on this. The guy's job ends after the screwing session and from that time on, it's the girl's job to carry, deliver and raise the brat. It's been that way for a million years and there is absolutely no reason to change now.

Surviving Pregnancy

You married or moved in with this nice, slim, shapely chick. Now she is so big that she could get her own zip code. If she stands between you and the sun, you think a total eclipse has occurred.

What can you do? I developed a technique to avoid looking at my repulsive mate for the last three months of pregnancy. I looked at her face only and imagined her old body from the neck down! It worked well and I survived this critical period of time very well.

Also, during this trying period, you will hear the saying, "There is nothing prettier than a pregnant woman." This is usually said by someone who has recently had a kid, is about to have a kid, or looks like they should have a kid. Completely disregard this statement. Don't take a chance looking at your lady to see if there could be some truth in it. I can assure you, it is completely false!

I have also wondered many times why pregnant women are allowed on the streets. There really should be a law that requires them to stay indoors during the last three months of their condition. Write your congressman today and suggest this law. Let's keep our country beautiful! God bless America!

OK, It's Here

You got through the birth. Now this invader is going to be around for quite a spell. You have to train your lady to do all the caring for this creature, or you will become Mr. Mom.

I can truthfully swear, with my hand on a stack of girlie books, that I *never*, yes, that's never, as in not even *once*, changed a diaper. I also never *ever* fed, burped, or got up with the little urchins during the night.

You have to be especially careful when your wife returns from the hospital *not* to help her. Women will try to get you to do this and that because they are "recuperating." Tell her you heard about Indian squaws who worked in the field until the baby was born, took a half-hour off, and then went back to the field to finish the day's work with the kid on their back!

If she can con you into helping in the beginning, it will never stop. She will use the sympathy routine to harass you into submission.

If you flatly say "no," you'll get static. The trick is to pretend to go along with her. When the baby screams at four a.m. and she says "please," get up, stagger around the room with your eyes closed, trip over a few things and head for the kitchen. Open a bottle of beer (pour most of it in the sink, so you don't kill the kid), put it in the bassinet with the kid and crash back into the bed. Your wife will immediately go check and find the suds instead of formula. This should be the end of her requests for you to act as surrogate mother.

Diapers! You have to have a cast-iron stomach and blocked sinuses to change a diaper. I wouldn't even stay in the same room with a diaper. In the good old days,

all fathers had a trick to eliminate the possibility of having to change diapers more than once. It was called "the safety pin trick," and it was very simple. In the process of changing your first diaper, you jabbed the little brat with the pin! He screamed bloody murder and the wife never asked you to change a diaper again.

Over the years, mothers must have gotten together to petition diaper manufacturers to eliminate the pin and thus the safety pin trick, because now diapers have space-age tapes. The diapers are foolproof, so you have to use a different ploy to get out of changing diapers.

The best one I have discovered is the puke method. You grab the kid, peel back the used diaper and while the good woman is not looking, stick your finger down your throat and puke in her lingerie drawer.

Tell her the old weak stomach is back in action, and there is no way you can ever change a diaper again. Immediately after your performance, plump your ass down in front of the TV to recuperate, and holler for her to bring you a cold brew. Recuperate in front of the TV for at least two hours.

The Alias

How many millions of times have you heard smelly, runny-nosed screaming little brats hollering "Daddy, Daddy, Daddy?" Picture this: you are at the grocery store (shopping mall, park, roller rink, etc.) with your little kid, who is running around trying to steal or break something in another area. If you are extremely handsome, charming and distinguished looking like me, you will probably encounter a beautiful girl, scantily dressed, all alone and hot-to-trot. She immediately engages you in chitchat with the ultimate goal of bedding you. Five minutes into this maneuver, your rotten brat appears and says, "Daddy, can I have ten bucks to buy some dope?"

She gasps, "Daddy? You're married, you bastard. Shove off!" Then she wiggles her nice round sexy rear off in pursuit of some more legitimate prey.

Now all this can be prevented by simply training your offspring to call you by your first name! I always insisted that my kids call me "Andy" instead of daddy for *safety* reasons, and these same reasons will work in convincing your spouse that the kids should call you by your first name instead of the dreaded word "Daddy."

Example 1—you are at a picnic, in a nice backyard with a pool. There are many families; 37 mommies, 35 daddies and 73 little mouths calling "Daddy," "Mommy," all day long. You immediately erase the word "daddy" from your mind. Then your two-year-old wanders over to the edge of the pool and *splash.* He yells "Daddy, Daddy," and you collect his life insurance the next week. If he had hollered "Andy, Andy," you would have responded, since you wouldn't tune out your own name.

23

His little life would have been saved and he would have probably grown up to become famous like Lee Harvey Oswald or Benedict Arnold.

Example 2—(even though example number 1 should convince her!). A child molester cruises along the curb near the school. Your sexy little brat appeals to this creep. He pulls over and says, "Your daddy asked me to pick you up and give you a ride home." The kid jumps in and is next seen on the side of a milk carton. If your kid had been taught that you are *always* referred to as "Andy," he would not have gotten into the car and you would still have him today, along with the bills for his braces, education, bail on Saturday night, and an abortion for his sixteen-year-old girlfriend.

Now let's return to our original story. You're with the sex goddess, the conversation is doing well, the gleam is still in her eye and the brat appears and says, "Andy, can I have ten bucks to buy some dope?" You say, "Here's twenty. Buy a double dose and live it up!"

The sex goddess says, "Who is that?" You answer, "my brother's kid," and head out with her for the nearest No-tell Motel!

Nice country we live in. God bless America!

KEEP OFF THE ASS!

The First Wife

Want to keep your old lady on her toes? Whenever you introduce her to friends, acquaintances or clients, do *not* say, "This is my wife, Evelyn." That will only lead your woman to believe that she is a permanent, indispensable fixture, and will always be around. Instead, say, "This is my first wife, Evelyn." This leads the lady into thinking that she is on probation and that if she does not perform well, you will be introducing someone else in a few months saying, "This is my second wife, so-and-so."

And don't just use the "first wife" title in introductions. Use it at all times, i.e., "This is my first wife's car," or "My first wife will be in to pick it up."

Play the numbers game with your mate and you will see an immediate change in attitude.

Political Power

Obviously you are more competent than your mate in evaluating political candidates, so all the important decisions regarding which lever to pull in the voting machine should be made by you. If you leave any decisions open regarding which candidate to vote for, she will undoubtedly vote for the pretty face even if he was just released from prison yesterday, is a known child molester, or is looney. You should handle this in one of two ways.

A blind person is allowed help in the voting booth. Get your wife a white cane and hold her by the arm. Take her in and tell the voting inspector she is blind. Go into the booth with her and pull down the levers for her.

The second method is a bit risky since it involves trust. You mark up a sample ballot and let her go in alone. The next day, when the winners are announced, get together with her at the kitchen table and see how the candidates fared that you mutually voted for. If she did not follow your instructions to the letter, she will triumphantly call your attention to the candidates she voted for who got elected.

Your first inclination may be to sentence her to several days of solitary confinement in the basement with a bread and water diet for disobeying you. I had such an experience when Tricky Dick was running for president and my first wife voted for him against my orders. She gloated the next day that *her* candidate won! I devised a novel way to punish her and I think it will work for you. Each year the local board of elections sends out a postcard to verify that the voter is still residing at the address used in the last election. When the card comes with your lady's name on it, write "deceased" and send it back. You should have seen the look on my wife's face when she showed up to vote the following November and the inspector told her she was dead!

To this day, she has never straightened it out. This is a nice country we live in. God bless America!

Boys' Night Out

Although your wife may not be extremely happy about your going out on the town with the boys, she will graciously allow it and even recommend it if you do the following:

When she whimpers, cries and stamps her feet at your plans to go out for a few beers with some of your gang, tell her you will stay home and invite your gang over! Don't invite them all—if there are some nice, quiet, well-behaved gentlemen, leave them out. Just invite the crazies, rowdies, sex maniacs, drunks and weirdos! Stock up on the booze, and liquor-up your pals as soon as they arrive.

You could even coordinate the guy's visit with your wife's family's visit, just for good measure. It will work wonders.

At one point in my marriage to my first wife, she com-

plained about my spending an hour or two at the neighborhood saloon with the guys. I was fortunate enough to be in contact with a few Indians (actually I think it was an entire tribe!), so I invited them over to my house for a glass or two of firewater. The chief tried to scalp my first wife, and a brave galloped away on my son's rocking horse, until it broke a leg when another Indian shot it! They made long-distance calls to the reservation and raided the refrigerator.

My first wife never again objected to my going out with the gang!

Give it a try, but be sure your homeowner's insurance is paid in case something gets out of control. After your wife cleans up the mess, you won't have to worry about her squawking again. Note: I was fortunate enough to have access to the Indians, but you may have to substitute a motorcycle gang, gypsies, crop-pickers, illegal aliens, or outpatients from the local mental ward!

Food

Yum-yum, or yuck-yuck!

Yum-yum, you grabbed one that has a body and knows how to cook. They say that "the way to a man's heart is through his stomach." That's close, but I think the way to a man's heart is really through the little thing right *below* his stomach! I've known many guys who ended up with a chick who couldn't even boil toast! (or is it water they're not supposed to be able to boil?)

What can be done? If you've got the beauty who avoids the kitchen like it was a foreign country, there is one solution. Live very close to a fast-food restaurant, a take-out delicatessen or within the delivery zone of a 30-minute pizza parlor.

In training the yum-yum chick (she's a looker and a cooker!), the trick is to get her to cook what you want. If you have ten favorite meals and she has six favorite meals, that means that you will be gagging down something you don't like six nights out of sixteen! There is absolutely no reason to eat something you don't enjoy but if you bitch about it, your chick may call you inconsiderate, selfish and other unprintable maledictions.

The trick is trying to find out in advance of plopping down at the table what she is going to serve for your feed tonight. If you find out that she is preparing her favorite porcupine stew which is not high on your list, about four o'clock that afternoon grab a sandwich from the deli near your office and eat it. When you get home, tell her you are famished, you could eat the south end of a skunk going north, you haven't had a bite all day, you were too busy to eat lunch, etc. When she puts the

porcupine stew in front of you, pick at it, push it around your plate, cut and stack it, salt and pepper it, but whatever you do, don't put any in your mouth! But don't say you don't like it, because she spent all day picking the needles out of the porcupines. If you say you don't like it, she may get a "headache" and you will have to refer to your little black book again tonight.

This method, if done correctly at all of her favorite meals, will eventually get the menu down to just your own favorites. You have all seen the finicky cat on the TV commercial. He puts his whiskers up in the air at the cheap cat food and ends up getting gourmet cat-chow. If it works for Morris, it will work for you.

Caution: Every once in a while your spouse will snap! When she spends hours over a hot microwave and then you fast, she goes berserk. Be ready to duck an airborne plateful of spaghetti.

My first wife created several murals on our dining room walls during her training period. I have often thought of visiting that apartment again and seeing if her spaghetti designs still cling to the rich purple walls!

Money

Money, bucks, rubles, bread, moolah, or what have you. It is said to be the root of all evil and it may well be. One important lesson that must be taught early to your female is that *you* are the banker. You control all the funds for everything: food, booze, vacations, clothes, living expenses. If she is working, she surrenders her measly paycheck to you. You dole out an allowance to cover her bus fare and hot dog lunches, plus $2.00 a week for unexpected items.

You must never let her know how much there is in the bank account, for women are prone to becoming extravagant when they think a surplus is available. If she thinks there's available cash, she may decide she needs new shoes when a new piece of cardboard in the sole would easily make the shoes last a few more months!

If she has access to the banking machine, you will have big problems. A trip to the Super Bowl is expensive and if you allow her to raid the nest-egg for every little event that she considers important (like her mother's thirtieth wedding anniversary or her retarded brother's graduation from reform school), the money will disappear like a fat girl in quicksand.

You should not have a joint bank account. The checks should be negotiable only by you. Although many partnerships start smoothly, many end on a sour note. If she has any control of the purse strings, she may someday disappear with the garbageman and leave you with an empty bank account.

Explain to her that your coexistence should be based on trust, and she should trust you with her funds. If she says anything about you trusting *her* with the key to

the vault, change the subject. Everyone knows men are better at handling the cash.

Refuse all initial requests from her for money. Shake your head violently from side to side, grimace, make weird sounds and roll your eyes back in your head. Walk from the room. Most times this will discourage her from asking again. If she does ask again and the request seems reasonable ("Can I have $3.00 for formula for the baby?"), you should try to reduce the amount. ("How about two bucks?") Make 'em beg!

I have always told my first wife that by teaching her to beg, I was preparing her for the future. If something ever happened to me, she would not have to starve. She would be experienced at begging!

If you are considering any investments, do not ever discuss the prospective investment with the old lady. Make the decision yourself, or rely on your broker or real estate agent. Women throw cold water on many good ideas. A friend of mine once had the chance to buy an old run-down gas station for twenty-five grand. The station sat on a mildly busy corner and had a good-sized lot. His wife took one look at it and raised hell. She told him that old gas stations weren't worth a nickel. Since he had made the mistake of mingling their funds and a good share of the bucks was hers, she insisted that he back out of the deal. He did, and a short while later the guy who bought the dumpy old gas station sold the property to a major motel chain for $150,000!

If ever there was a reason for justifiable homicide, this sure was it. Keep control of the cash!

Her Friends

First of all, she *does not* need any male friends. You know what guys are after—you're a guy! Eliminate all of her male friends immediately. It's easy to do. If they call on the phone and you answer, just say "no, she's not here right now. She's at the doctor. They have this new treatment for herpes . . ." That should do it.

The old lady's girlfriends require a different approach. Carefully evaluate them. Are they good looking? Do they like you? Is there a chance that they may be able to fill in when your wife is sick, or out of town? Would they side with the old lady if an argument arises, or would they take your side? Rate their importance to *you*, and then dispense with any who serve no practical purpose.

Getting rid of them is easy. You can just be plain rude, or point-blank tell them you don't like them and that if you see them around again, you may punch their ugly faces in, or run them over with your car. Girls scare easily. Trying to look a little deranged when you speak to them and having a little booze on your breath is a very convincing technique.

Another good trick is to answer the phone when the unwanted chick calls and the old lady is not home. Say "Just a minute," and then partially cover the mouthpiece and say, "It's that idiot again. Do you want to talk to her?" Then uncover the mouthpiece and say in a real nice voice, "She must have gone out. I'll tell her you called." I don't think your wife's friend will call again.

Your chick doesn't need these people around anyway. They are just excess baggage. All she needs is for you to be happy ever after!

The Backup

Do you have a spare tire in your trunk? Is there a key under your doormat? Do parachutists have an emergency chute? Are Boy Scouts prepared? Yes, yes, yes, and yes. So of course you need a backup for the old girl. What if she chokes on a chicken bone, gets hit by a car, drops her hair dryer in the bathtub or otherwise goes to the happy hunting ground without giving you proper notice?

The kids will be all alone with no one to tuck them in at night—unless you have a backup that can immediately come to your rescue and move in before the old lady's body even gets cold.

The backup is especially important when you have little brats, but she is also important if you will be alone. You need someone to pick up your socks, hang up your jeans, and keep you happy at night.

Every guy should keep a chick on the back-burner for an emergency, and I am sure that your lady could not possibly be angry if you explain how the backup is necessary for the health and well-being of the little ones (or you).

If you are really good at selecting the backup, you will find one the same size as your old lady, so that she can utilize the clothes in the closet, thus saving you many, many bucks.

Cultivating a backup may take some time but if you really love your family, it will be worth it. I am sure that the sacrifice in time and cash that it takes to keep the backup on standby will pay big dividends in the end. It's ideal if she and the main lady are friends because then you can bring her right into the house. That way,

if she is ever needed, the backup will be familiar with the layout and mechanics of the household and not need much training.

Some civilizations allow a guy to have several mates simultaneously and, if this practice were legalized in the good old USA, it probably would make a lot of ladies and guys happy. I say ladies because they, too, would benefit because they could share the chores (two ladies means they only cook one-half as much; wash one-half as much, etc.).

Life Insurance

As every agent will tell you, you *need* life insurance for you and your wife. It's a good thing to have adequate coverage on the old lady because if she croaks, the bucks will come in handy. But consider this—you are going to spend good, hard cash that you could be using for booze or what have you to insure yourself so that the old lady can have a good time after you're gone! Does that make sense? What really makes sense is to insure her life and not your own. If you bite the dust and don't have a nickel's worth of insurance, she'll do okay because you have taught her how to beg (see "Money" chapter). Don't put your hard-earned bucks on the line for your insurance; use it to get great coverage on her.

If the little lady wants coverage on you, she can take a few bucks out of her allowance and pay for it herself as my first wife did. Keep a limit on the amount of insurance that she buys on you. There have been many cases of the wife sprinkling a little rat poison in the hubby's porridge when she became unhappy with the old man. You don't want to tempt the little darling with a huge bounty on your demise.

Wheels

Many guys think it better to keep the little lady off the streets to reduce the chance of her getting too far from the nest. Actually, it's more productive to get her a jalopy so that she can run errands, leaving you with more free time. While you are at work, she can be out picking up a keg of beer, some bait or ammo for your hunting trip, some dry ice to pack your steaks in, etc.

Use caution when picking out wheels for her. If you get her a red sports car or a convertible and she hits the highway, she will attract guys like flies to crap. Remember, she fell for *your* line when you met her. If she is tooling around with the top down and her long blond hair flying in the breeze, some smooth talker may follow her and sweet-talk her into something that you disapprove of.

Her vehicle should be conservative. Just because you drive a Rolls, there is no reason for her to have one. If she complains that you are cruising around in a brand-new Cadillac Eldorado Biarritz (like I have) and she is driving a Jeep with a plow (like my first wife drives), just explain that if you bought another Cadillac for her, the IRS would certainly audit your tax return for the past twenty-seven years.

If you live very close to the grocery, liquor and bait stores, you may even consider not getting her a full-fledged car. Just get her a moped with a basket on it, a 10-speed bike, or a little red wagon she can pull down to the store on your errands.

Another important item is a personalized license plate for her flivver. She may want "SEXY LADY," "TRY ME," "I'M GOOD," "WILLING," "SINGLE," or some other

imaginative handle. Ignore her requests and get her a plate that says "MOM" or "ANDY'S CHICK." (Put your name in place of Andy's because there are already twelve "ANDY'S CHICK" plates.)

You may want to add one finishing touch to the little lady's wheels that will be a good turnoff for many guys who pull alongside your chick on the freeway. Get a kid's car seat and permanently attach it where it will be easily seen from passing cars. When she questions why you put this stupid thing in her car when neither one of you have a brat and both of you hate kids, mention that you read about using kiddie seats to hold fragile products (bottled beer, pretzels, etc.) on shopping trips so that a fast stop does not damage them.

P.S.—to keep her from taking this nice clunker you have provided her with and abandoning you, drill a hole in the gas tank about one-quarter of the way up so that the tank won't hold any more than a quarter tank of fuel. She can get to the store or tackle shop and back, but she won't get away.

Employment

A woman's place is in the home, but . . . if she has some skill like dancing, selling real estate, or hanging wallpaper, she could easily handle this work and still be home in time to do the chores around the house before you get home. To help her, you should do all the banking and bookkeeping for her. Have her give you the dough as soon as she comes home on Friday night. You can dole out her allowance for the next week and, if she has been real good, slip her an extra buck or two. This will be an incentive to her to produce more each week.

Keep an eye on her associates because they may realize what a gold mine you have going and try to jump your claim.

Vacations

It's a proven fact that a vacation is necessary from time to time to enhance your mind and body. You must, however, train your lady to go to the spot of your dreams and not to some place that she picks.

I started early with my bride. Before I was married, I had raced or been a spectator at an annual Labor Day State Fair Championship auto race for many years. My wife was not overly eager to go to the races and we were getting married the Saturday before Labor Day. I suggested that we spend our honeymoon at the state fair and didn't mention the Labor Day race until we got there. For the next twenty years, I suggested that we relive our honeymoon and go to the fair for sentimental purposes. To this day, I have never missed the state fair championship race!

Get the idea? Tie the vacation at the Super Bowl or Kentucky Derby to a sentimental occasion, anniversary, or something, so you can repeat it, and the old lady will go along with it. Maybe every tenth year you can go to some place that really turns her on if she bitches about going to all the places you like.

Trust

You have probably seen this word on the front of a bank. Do you trust your bank? Has it ever taken your car away in the middle of the night when you were a payment or so behind? This word also appears on much of the legal tender of our government. Do you trust our government, the government that brought you Watergate, Cambodia, Vietnam, Richard Nixon or double-digit inflation?

What I am trying to make clear is that you should never trust your lady. Never. No matter how good she seems, always keep your eyes open. Look past what she says. Keep track of the mileage on her moped. If she says she is going to the shopping mall and it is three miles away and her mileage jumps to twelve for the day, she may be meeting some guy at the local "No-Tell" Motel. Listen carefully to every word she says. Usually she will slip up. For example, "This is just like the wallpaper at the Grecian Room." Did you ever take her to dinner at the Grecian Room? You get the idea.

I had an interesting experience several years ago. I had gained a little weight and my waist went from a 34 to a 36. Nothing big. I still looked dazzling. My BVDs were a little frayed from changing them several times a day, so my first wife decided to replenish my underwear drawer. The 34s were plenty comfortable for me but she bought 36s. So as not to make a big thing out of my slight weight gain, she washed the new 36s and put them in with my underwear. The next day, as I pulled on my drawers, I noticed a 36 label! What would you have thought? The same thing I thought. Some snake had been with the old lady and, in departing had

44

grabbed the 34 and left the 36. I didn't say a word to her, but I had a pal who was a private eye stake out the joint and follow my first wife everywhere she went for a week. She checked out clean. My next step was to confront her, and she told me the story about buying the new drawers for me. Better to be safe than sorry, but the new underwear cost me $350, considering what I paid my friend to follow her!

Since I couldn't afford to trust her, and I obviously couldn't afford unauthorized purchases, I trained my first wife to give me the receipts for all her transactions. So she would suspect nothing, I told her that this was for tax purposes.

Housework

Many girls will suggest a plan, especially if they are working, to share domestic chores. Again, if you point-blank refuse, you will have to suffer her harassment and possibly have to get out the black book.

First you have to agree. "Hey, that's a great idea. If I'm home before you, I will start dinner." Then be sure *not* to be home first. Stop for a drink or two, or stop at your girlfriend's house on the way home. Next time, get home ahead of her and actually start the porridge perking. Find the biggest kettle and make enough for Christ and the Twelve Apostles; be sure some boils over into the burners, and also track some across the floor. When she comes home, act really happy, and tell her you made plenty in case she was very hungry. If you can burn the feast a little around the edges, it will add to the desired effect. She will probably shortly decide that you are not suited to being a chef.

Now, housework is more than just cooking. There are dishes to wash, the house to clean, laundry, etc. Let's take them one at a time:

Dishes: Are they precious heirlooms her mother left her? Hee, hee, ha ha, you get the idea already, you little devil. If she doesn't discharge you after the first dish hits the floor, try this: put them away carefully, very carefully. I have put some dishes away that my first wife still couldn't find after five years! I recommend putting them behind the big plate, under the bowls, under the pots and pans, etc.

House cleaning: The vacuum cleaner is a good instrument with which to begin your project. Does your wife's cat have a long tail? Does the old lady leave her panty hose on the bedroom rug? All these items fit into the vacuum-cleaner hose. Does your wife have a favorite picture hanging on the wall, like a graduation picture from Keene Valley Consolidated High School? Dust it vigorously, until it falls off the wall. Does her collection of ornate teacups need dusting, too?

Laundry: This one is easy. Put all the colored and white clothes into the machine, add one full box of soap and start the hot-water cycle. When I did this, the blizzard of soap suds filled the main sewer, backed up through the house sewer, went up the downspouts to the roof gutters and gently floated down from the roof in the form of big white bubbles. Lawrence Welk would have felt at home!

Note: Be sure you combine only the lady's items of different colors because if your white designer underwear turns pink and you undress at your girlfriend's house, she might think you're a fag.

If you do all of the above and she still asks you to help with the domestic chores, you should obtain psychiatric help for your lady immediately.

Another interesting method of getting the housework done and not tying up your time or your lady's is to hire a domestic. You don't have to be rich to hire this type of help because they are usually cheap. My first one was a nice looking, Jamaican girl named Olive. She was supplied by a firm that specializes in importing these people by finding jobs for them, arranging passports and work papers and doing all the legal hocus-pocus. They must have a job to come to the good old USA. If they screw up, it's back on the boat. It's something like legal slavery. You should interview several and, if you still have the plywood template (see "The Right Stuff" chapter), you should get it out again for these interviews.

I had Olive for three years. She took care of my kids, did household chores, cleaned one of my rooming houses, rented apartments and did other things I liked. One caution—there is a thing called a "green card." Once your sexy slave gets her green card, she can quit and get a higher paying, minimum-wage job at the local Holiday Inn. A good technique is to have all your domestic's mail sent directly to your address "just so it doesn't get lost." Then you can keep an eye out for the green card. I accidentally misplaced Olive's green card for eleven months.

Yard Work

If you are a healthy red-blooded male, you can probably think of more important tasks than pushing a mower or pulling a rake on Saturday morning. You can go to the beach, play basketball with the guys or just hang around the house watching the old lady cut the grass.

She will be very upset if you just say, "Go out and cut the grass." As we have demonstrated in previous chapters, you must get her to do it on her own. Mention that it's really good exercise, that the sun will work wonders on her lovely skin, and how firm her legs always look when she does this kind of work. Within five minutes, you will see her in her bikini, pushing the mower across the yard.

The same thing will work with pool cleaning, window washing and other outside chores. Don't make her work too hard. About every hour, tell her to take a break and run into the house where it's cool and fetch you a brew.

The Big One!

What do you think the biggest cause of marital problems is today? Husband running around? Wife fooling around? Money or lack of it? In-laws butting in? Sex or lack of it? None of these. A recent secret study done in conjunction with marriage counselors, divorce lawyers, and gypsy fortune-tellers revealed that the number one cause—the straw that broke the camel's back—was *the toilet seat!* This has caused more problems in civilized America than all others combined. One of the rewards you are going to reap from parting with your bucks for this book is the answer to this big problem. A conservative estimate of how many times you will have to lift the toilet seat, if you are a normal gent with

normal kidneys and you hit the brew four times a day and stay married twenty years, is the astounding figure of 39,200 times! That's a lot of lid lifting.

Here is the secret. Have the old lady lift the seat *after* she goes! Then it's up when you feel the need! Isn't that simple? Why didn't you think of that? Train the little lady to do this and there is no more reason for her to bitch, unless of course, she makes a pit stop in the night, doesn't turn the light on and forgets that the seat is up. But then, that's no fault of your own!

Once you train her, you will have a lot of time on your hands since lifting that seat would have taken about 50 hours of your time. Now you can enjoy that time with the boys down at the corner bar or chasing some young thing.

In-Laws

Unless your lady is a product of two test tubes who got together in a laboratory, she will have a mommy and daddy. Even if you got her straight out of an orphanage, she has a mommy and daddy somewhere. One thing that all mothers-in-law and daddies-in-law have in common is that they will not like you! You are too tall or too short, too poor or too rich, too dumb or too smart for their precious little girl. Even if you come from royalty, 99 percent of the in-laws will still think you are not good enough for their little girl. I once knew a nuclear power engineer who made more in one day than I made in two weeks. He picked up a hooker on Halloween and fell in love with her. The hooker's daddy was a gambler and her mother a dope addict, but when they met my friend, they looked down on him. He wasn't good enough for their little girl!

How do you win? You don't. You don't even bother trying. There is no practical purpose in trying to impress your in-laws. You're only after your chick, not the whole family. (Of course, there may be some exception if your mother-in-law is really good looking or your old lady's sister is a "10".)

Any time or bucks spent trying to impress your in-laws is counterproductive and can be better spent on pleasurable items for you and the fox. I would seriously say that in twenty-plus years of married life, I have probably never done anything to impress my in-laws. I've been civil and reasonably pleasant but I have not gone overboard. There is no reason to. One kind of Joe gets trapped into trying to please the old lady and her parents. He runs around doing errands for the mother-in-law, fixes the father-in-law's clunker and does other assorted chores to prove he is a good son-in-law. He runs himself ragged trying to impress "mom and pop," but I guarantee that if you ask mom and pop what they think of the son-in-law, they will say, "She should have married so-and-so instead."

My in-laws live 470 miles away and we visit them once each year. I think that this is a good distance and the frequency of visits just right.

The Hacienda

If you can find a chick whose old man just died or went to prison for life leaving his old lady with a mansion on the ocean, mortgage paid in full, fully furnished and two-car garage with two cars already in it, you have struck it rich. The odds of this happening are remote, so you should make contingency plans for a roof over your head. Why is planning necessary? Simple. You may want to live close to your office so you can sleep a little later each morning but your lady may want to live close to where she works so she can sleep late. Since she works on the lower east side and you work on the upper west side, it will be impossible to accommodate both of you. This book is devoted to pleasing you, so let's proceed in getting a pad to your liking.

Get a copy of the local paper and scan it for lower east side muggings, rapes, robberies and murders. Read

them aloud. Make a big deal out of these crimes. Mention that, if you lived on the lower east side, you would have to jack your car up every night and bring in the hub caps and wheels so they wouldn't be stolen during the night.

At the same time, find nice bars, clubs, parks and beaches on the upper west side and take her to these every day. Make her feel at home on your turf and she will be quite receptive to looking for accommodations close to your office.

The next thing you will have to do after getting her to agree on the area is to get her to like the apartment or house you want to live in. On this point, you are really lucky. I have spent the past fifteen years as a real-estate broker, getting people to buy something they didn't want, so I can give you some exceptional insight on this one.

When you find something you like for various reasons (girl next door has big jugs, close to a bar, football stadium a couple of blocks away, etc.), you will have to impress her on the property. The process is simple and known in the real estate business as "reduce to ridiculous." You don't actually meet her objection head-on and argue the point. You just reduce her objection to a ridiculous level.

When you find the ideal apartment in an "optional clothing" condo project filled with gorgeous young ladies and she says she may not feel comfortable without her clothes, mention that she will be saving many, many hours by not having to do as much laundry and a substantial amount in dry-cleaning expense!

When you find the ideal house next to a soap opera starlet whose sunbathing area is under your bedroom window but your lady says the kitchen is too small, come back with "I purposely looked for a place with a small kitchen because it will save you time and steps in preparing a meal." How could she turn this place down when you have looked out for her interests!

Hair

Have you ever noticed how good the old lady looks *before* she goes to the hairdresser? For some reason ladies think that the beautician can work miracles with scissors that they could not perform themselves. They somehow equate the skill of the hairdresser with that of a brain surgeon. If you think back, you will not recall a single case of your girl looking better after she returned from the beauty shop. The best thing to do is forbid her from going to any beauty shop.

If that doesn't work, you will have to revert to psychological warfare. When she returns and walks through the door, scream as loud as you can and keep screaming until the other tenants or neighbors call the cops. Tell her if she ever scares you again like that, you will kill her. Tell her you want the name of the guy who did this to her and immediately call your lawyer. Tell him you want to start a lawsuit because some idiot has disfigured your lady.

If she went to the hairdresser because she was planning on going with you to some important function, leave her home and go without her. This will usually do the trick.

57

Fat Farms

When the old lady gets bored or when she looks in the mirror and sees a little fat on a spot that was boney before, she may be tempted to join a health club. If she is pleasing to you the way she is, don't allow her to waste money on a membership to one of the karate schools, exercise clubs, or aerobic dance classes. They cost money and deprive you of your lady's companionship while she is sweating off three pounds. There is also a chance that she may get the urge to try out her new-found muscles; for example, exercising her pelvic muscles with the assistance of the muscle-bound instructor.

Keep her out of these joints unless she really needs exercise. If she gets a bulge where you don't want one, by all means, ship her out to the fat farm, but try this: have her join under a phoney name. Then when she has dropped her excess baggage, she can quit and they won't be able to collect the balance of her membership.

Before you try sending her to the fat farm, you should consider something more productive, like having her deliver the morning newspaper. The walking, stair-climbing and paper carrying will possibly burn off more calories than the jumping jacks with the fat ladies down at the spa. You will also be getting a few extra bucks from her endeavors and this can be put away for a rainy day or a night on the town.

The Bailout

Some say all good things must come to an end and this may be true. The problem with things coming to an end is that sometimes you end up with less than you started with, and that's not right. It's a good idea to sit down with your lawyer and draw up an agreement to be signed by you and the chick at an early date. However, many times the sex drive short-circuits the brain and this legal aspect gets bypassed.

There are many complications when a union breaks up, but a big one is bucks. She wants all of them. She may have come into this thing with $5.98, but she wants to go out with the vault.

I'm going to give you a tip or two on how to keep the coins. Let's say you and the lady jointly own a pad and things aren't going that well. It's a shack worth a hundred grand, and she probably would walk away with fifty big ones if the judge got involved. I had a friend in this exact situation. He devised a plan. He was real nice to the lady. He wined and dined her. He brought home presents. He became the ideal husband. He took her off guard. He told her the old house was not good enough for his lady. She should have something bigger, in a better neighborhood, with a pool, etc. He contacted a local realtor, listed his house and began looking at nicer homes. A buyer was found for his joint and he "told" his wife that they were buying that "nice place we saw last Sunday." She was elated. She began packing and preparing for the move to the palace. Unbeknownst to her, he had not even made an offer on the palace and had absolutely no intention of buying another home. After the closing on the present house, the attorney gave

60

him a check made out to him and his wife for a hundred grand. He had his wife endorse it so he "could give it to the realtor as down payment on the palace." He then took it to the bank, cashed it, and was soon on his way to a warmer climate with his girlfriend.

I'm not suggesting that you cheat the old lady out of anything, but this scheme sure worked well for my friend.

Gifts

They cost money! Money you may otherwise divert to goodies like a new pair of jeans, a motorcycle or a trip to Daytona for spring break or a night out. Many guys spoil their ladies with lavish gifts, flowers, candy and other junk.

It's really not a good idea to give the ladies anything. You will spoil them, if you do. In reality if you spend five dollars once a year instead of $20 a week, the five-dollar gift will be appreciated *more*. The reasoning behind this is that the frequency of the weekly or monthly gifts lulls her into expecting something. If you ever don't bring home the weekly or monthly gift, she will actually be mad. When you bring home the five-buck bottle of champagne once a year, she will be ecstatic! She didn't expect it and will probably reward you more for this measly bottle of booze than if you had spent $500 bucks over the past year in gratuities.

Keep the gift cheap and only once or twice a year!

Pets

I know you already have one, but I'm talking about the animal kind of pet, not the human kind. Over the years, my first wife put up with various live things that attracted my fancy from a coyote dog that I trapped on a mountain side to a couple of members of the lion family that I imported from Ethiopia. Needless to say, my first wife was not very happy having to clean up, feed and sometimes defend herself from attacks.

The first thing you must do, if you are going to introduce an animal into the family, is not warn anyone about your plan. If you ask the old lady about bringing home an ocelot, she will vehemently object. The way to do it is just spring it on her. While she is out shopping, bring the pet in and get it situated. Usually an animal will lay claim to its territory and when the old lady gets home, it will be her that has to prove that she belongs. The bigger the animal, the more authority it exerts, so keep this in mind when you select a pet.

Another good thing about a pet is that it can keep an eye (or claw, jaw, trunk or fang) on the old lady when you are not around. I once had a pair of white German shepherds who would not let anyone in the house while I was not home. I think this kept my first wife on the straight-and-narrow for quite some time.

You will get maximum enjoyment of your pet by having the old lady do the pet chores—bathing the gorilla, emptying the lion's litter box, or whatever is a dirty and hazardous job.

Feeding the critters must be done on a regular basis or they may eat you! You can get the lady to take care of these chores by just not doing them yourself. If the litter box has an unpleasant aroma to it, either don't go home until she empties it, or put a little cotton up your nose so you don't smell it. Feeding is easy—just ask her to feed the kitty *today*. Animals are smart. Once she feeds them, the animals will go to her every time they get hungry. If she does not feed them, they will claw, bite or bark until she does.

After pets are around for awhile, they and the lady will be inseparable.

The Tube

Murders have occurred over "what are we going to watch tonight!" I solved this problem with the addition of a second TV. My number one TV is a huge, color, rear projection set with stereo sound and a 48-inch screen. This is set up in my living room opposite a contoured, adjustable, made-to-fit-my-perfect-body easy chair.

When my first wife and I disagree on the channel of the evening, the problem is easily solved. She retreats to the bedroom, props herself up with three pillows and an empty beer case, flips on the 12-inch used black-and-white TV and enjoys her favorite trash.

This is the best way to handle the channel problem, and if you check the pawnshops, I am sure you will find the ideal TV for the missus.

Decisions, Decisions

Some important decisions are required every day. If these decisions are really important, you should make them without ever consulting the old lady. If she is involved in any way, shape, or form in making decisions, she will screw up. Women are not good decision-makers, and they never will be for the reason that they are too easily influenced by emotional or personal feelings. Make all the decisions yourself and if she says anything, say, "I booked us on this ski trip because I know you will like it" or "I bought this riding mower because you really deserve the best."

Let her think that you were looking out for her. If you really want to go crazy, let her make a simple decision once in a while. "Should we go to the show at 7:15 or 8:30?" "Should we paint the dining room white or off-white?"

Beware, for there are dangers inherent in such a closed-mouth system. I kept one decision to myself several years ago, and one of my clients ended up in jail. I had just purchased a house for my first wife and I to reside in and we had moved in. My first wife was busy planting daisies and hanging curtains. In my business as a realtor, I discovered a house I liked better and bought it without mentioning it to my wife. This meant I would have to sell the house my spouse was sprucing up. I decided I would not mention the proposed sale until the little lady had finished doing her doll-up job. A client of mine mentioned that he was looking for a pad, so I told him to "take a look at 50 Tyler Street, but don't mention that it's for sale to anyone." He parked his Harley Davidson down the street and began walking around the

66

yard. My wife promptly had him arrested, and I was quite surprised when my client called me from the jail! But everything worked out well. I got him out, he bought the house and I moved to the new residence. Quite possibly I should have informed the old lady about the proposed sale, but normally I don't second-guess where she is concerned.

Conclusion

Girls are certainly nice things to have around. Keep them in good working order and well trained, and many will last a lifetime. Never let up on the training and refresher courses. If you do, it will be like letting the inmates run the asylum. A little training will go a long way toward having a happy home life.

If your lady becomes untrainable, runs amuck, or doesn't fit in with your current program, just keep in mind there are thousands more out there and new ones are being made every day. They take some effort and work, but the alternatives (no cook, cleaning or bed-warmer) are not attractive unless you are limp-wristed.

Good Luck!